快速中文

Fast Chinese!

Most Useful Chinese Nouns!

Traditional Chinese Version: Volume 1

by YiXuan Li

Fast Chinese!
fastchinesebooks@gmail.com

No unauthorized photocopying

ISBN: 9798631173958
Independently published
Copyrighted material

**Fast Chinese!
Most Useful Chinese Nouns!
Volume 1**

CONTENTS

INSTRUCTION

PRONUNCIATION

CHINESE NOUNS by TOPIC

Introduction

In the Fast Chinese! Most Useful Chinese Nouns! book, you'll learn strong foundations for some of the most common nouns needed to advance your reading, writing and speaking of Mandarin Chinese! In order to become a fluent and advanced speaker of the Chinese language, understanding of these nouns is very important.

Along with each noun, example sentences are shown in the form of a question and answer, which also serves as a means to see how grammar is used accurately in daily life. The nouns compiled here are categorized alphabetically and by topic in order to assist with retention and learning. It's important to know that Chinese nouns are not indicated as singular and plural like in many other languages, but there are relatively simple ways to show this distinction. One of the biggest hurdles is to understand and incorporate "measure words", which are a necessary component of proper Mandarin Chinese. The **Fast Noun Tutorial** section of this book goes into further detail about Chinese nouns and their proper usage.

There are over 300 example sentences for all of the given vocabulary, and all of the nouns are highlighted in bold for both the Chinese characters and *pinyin*. These books were written with input from actual Chinese learners who were asked the question, "What do you wish you'd known earlier in your Chinese learning process?" With that in mind, the information and details presented here aim to remedy things that are often overlooked or taken for granted by teachers, and to expedite the progress of students learning Chinese!

How to use this book

Once you have a firm understanding of the pronunciation of the shown *pinyin*, you'll find that learning the characters and meanings are surprisingly easy-- only requiring a bit of repetition before you get the hang of it. It's very important to get your tones correct, as it's one of the pillars of proper Mandarin communication. It's best to start slow and be sure to speak each syllable distinctly. This is especially true when starting out as to avoid developing bad habits. Be sure each and every syllable is pronounced clearly with the appropriate tone.

Both constant use and review are crucial, so try to incorporate these common nouns into your daily speech as much as possible. Start with simple sentences, negative statements, questions, and references to singular and plural (if / when they're required). In daily conversation, most ideas are conveyed via simple sentences, which is what you should aspire to when starting out or incorporating new vocabulary. The focus should be on QUALITY over QUANTITY in order to solidify your foundation. This includes pronunciation, as well as proper word order / usage of nouns and measure words.

Simplicity is the aim of this book. Instead of weighing down the student with massive amounts of over-explanation, we've kept the focus on common nouns and useful examples, the kind that come up in daily life. These are things that many advanced students say, "I wish I'd known sooner in my own studies".

Each noun is grouped by topic and listed alphabetically with the English meaning, large traditional Chinese characters, and then the *hanyu pinyin* pronunciation. Examples are given for each noun in the form of a question and answer, with the associated "Measure Word" used when natural and appropriate for native speakers of Mandarin Chinese. Pay attention to the Noun-Measure Word pairings.

These practical examples show the Chinese characters for familiarity, a line of pinyin to aid with pronunciation, and then an English translation. Nouns are bolded to make them stand out. Of note is that the English is translated as it is commonly spoken in casual conversation (colloquially), which is how the Chinese sounds to a native Mandarin speaker as well. Our aim is to avoid "textbook sounding" speech that is unnatural or uncommon.

Practicing speaking these "blocks" of language should aid with fluency and retention, making your speech much more natural and uniform. The goal is to start using Chinese nouns and language correctly and immediately, covering various topics from daily life. This is exactly what we all want: Fast Chinese!

Fast Chinese!: Fast Noun Tutorial

What are nouns? In Chinese, 名詞 (míng cí) are the words used to express people, places, living creatures, objects, qualities, ideas, or states. Going further, we can organize them into different types: proper and common nouns, time nouns, and nouns for position / location. It's easy to see why they're absolutely necessary for effective communication. In Mandarin Chinese, nouns can be utilized in several important ways--which should all be explored and understood—but at a very basic level, one needs to be able to use them in singular / plural forms, as well as paired with suitable quantifiers (see "Measure Words" section, below). In the following sections, we've quickly outlined some core information a student of Mandarin Chinese needs in order to properly express the language naturally and efficiently.

Endings / Suffixes

Recognizing Nouns: Many two-syllable nouns in Chinese have the character zi (子, originally meaning "child") as the second word, which makes them easy to identify in speech and writing. Other possible second characters include 頭 / 兒* (tóu / er*). *The latter is more common in mainland China and simplified Mandarin. Examples:

Suffix	Example Nouns
子	椅子 (yǐ zi, chair), 鏡子 (jìng zi, mirror), 桌子 (zhuō zi, table)
頭	斧頭 (fǔ tóu, axe), 罐頭 (guàn tóu, can), 彈頭 (dàn tóu, warhead)
兒	男孩兒 (nán hái er, boy), 花兒 (huā er, flower), 馬兒 (mǎ er, horse)

Reduplication

"Reduplication" is a fancy way of saying that a word repeats. In Chinese, while verbs and adjectives are often repeated for various purposes, nouns generally are not. Some children will reduplicate nouns, and this gives their speaking a "cute" feel to it, but basically it should be avoided. This doubling of a noun is akin to "baby talk". As examples:

Reduplicated Noun	Meaning
兔兔	tù tù, "a bunny"
狗狗	gǒu gǒu, "a doggy"
貓貓	māo māo, "a kitty"

PRONOUNS

In Chinese, these are known as 代詞 (dài cí). In common usage, pronouns replace regular nouns and proper nouns in order to avoid repetition of words and to sound more natural. Simply put, we'll look at two of the most common types of pronouns: **personal pronouns** (he, she, we, they, etc.), and **demonstrative pronouns** (this, that, etc.).

Pronouns fit into the language the same way nouns do, we just have to be sure to use the right type. This is usually quite intuitive: if you refer to a person, use a personal pronoun like "he" or "she", while inanimate objects use "it".

Some good news? For the pronouns "he / she / it", the pronunciation is all the same in spoken Chinese (tā), so referring to a third person or object doesn't really require gender differentiation when talking. The gender of the character is only required in reading and writing.

Pronoun Reference Chart:

Pronoun / 代詞 / dài cí	Chinese / 中文 / zhōng wén	Pinyin / 拼音 / pīn yīn
I / me	我	wǒ
you	你 (m) / 妳 (f) / 您 (polite)	nǐ (m)/ nǐ (f)/ nín (pol)
He / him	他	tā
she / her	她	tā
it	它 / 牠 / 祂	tā
We / us	我們	wǒmen
You (plural)	你們 (m) / 妳們 (f)	nǐmen (m)/ nǐmen (f)
They / them	他們 / 她們 / 它們 / 牠們	tāmen/ tāmen/ tāmen/ tāmen

*those highlighted in gray are less commonly seen / used.

SINGULAR & PLURAL / 單數 & 複數 / dān shù & fù shù

We love sharing good news, so here's some more: for the most part, Chinese nouns don't need to worry about being plural; most singular and plural noun forms are the same! We'll say that again: **singular and plural nouns are generally identical in Chinese!** There are a few exceptions to this, but once learned, you can go back to enjoying the simplicity of expressing yourself with the simple grammar of Chinese! In English, we'll add an "-s" or "-es" ending to a noun to indicate more than one, which is not the case for this language. After learning the new vocabulary word and its pronunciation: that's it! For instance, the noun for "book", below, is the same whether there is one (書 , shū) or many (書 , shū).

One book.	一本書	yī běn **shū**
Many books.	很多本書	hěn duō běn **shū**

Grammar: Numbers

Most basically, numbers before a noun show how many there are of something, no matter if it's one or many.

| I bought one cup of coffee. | 我買了一杯咖啡 | wǒ mǎi le yī bēi kā fēi |
| I bought three cups of coffee. | 我買了三杯咖啡 | wǒ mǎi le sān bēi kā fēi |

DEMONSTRATIVE PRONOUNS: 這 / 那

這 (zhè, "this"), and 那 (nà, "that") can be made plural by adding 些 (xiē), resulting in: 這些 (zhè xiē, "these") and 那些 (nà xiē, "those"). These are the most common ways of plural noun expression, and they're quite intuitive and simple to master with minimal practice.

This	這	zhè
That	那	nà
These	這些	zhè xiē
Those	那些	nà xiē

Grammar: "ALL": 都

Another way of indicating multiple versions of something is having the word 都 (dōu, "all") immediately after the noun in a sentence. Its inclusion lets the listener know that there is more than one of the noun. An example:

| The car is broken. | 車子壞掉 | chē zi huài diào |
| The cars are all broken. | 車子都壞掉 | chē zi **dōu** huài diào |

Grammar: "EVERY": 每

In a similar way, the word 每 (měi, "every") added before each Measure Word and noun pairing (see "**Measure Words**" section, below) shows that the speaker is referring to more than one of something, simply by using the word "every". 每 (měi, "every") is used with 都 (dōu, "all", see previous section) to show emphasis of this.

Every piece of clothing is damaged.	每件衣服都破掉	měi jiàn yī fú dōu pò diào

The 們 Suffix

The plural indicator 們 (men) has some usage, but mostly with personal pronouns. For example, the pronoun "we / us" is the combination of 我 (wǒ, "I, me") with 們 , in order to create 我們 (wǒmen, "we" / "us"). See the pronoun reference chart, **above** for more details.

Nouns representing humans can also be made plural by the addition of the character 們. The word 朋友 (péng you, "friend") can be made into 朋友們 (péngyou men, "friends"), but this is somewhat optional, so don't think of it as a concrete rule.

POSSESSION: 的

Both nouns and pronouns can all be modified to show "possession" by adding 的 (de). This is very useful for showing not only ownership, but also close associations and references between things.

Possessive pronoun	Chinese / 中文 / zhōng wén	Pinyin / 拼音 / pīn yīn
my / mine	我的	wǒ de
your / yours	你的 (m) / 妳的 (f)	nǐ de / nǐ de
his/ his	他的	tā de
her / hers	她的	tā de
it/its	它的	tā de
our/ours	我們的	wǒ men de
your / yours (plural)	你們的 (m) / 妳們的 (f)	nǐmen de / nǐmen de
their / theirs	他們的 / 她們的 / 它們的	tā men de/ tā men de/ tā men de

Objects can use this as well, which shows "what's" thing you're referring to. Examples:

The monkey's ears.	猴子的耳朵	hóu zi **de** ěr duo
The restaurant's door.	餐廳的大門	cān tīng **de** dà mén

An exception to this is close personal / familial relationships with personal pronouns (most commonly family members), when 的 is optional, and can be omitted. For instance:

My father.	我的爸爸	wǒ de bà ba
My father. (omitted 的, but same meaning)	我爸爸	wǒ bà ba

MEASURE WORDS / 量詞

These "classifiers" are known as 量詞 (liàng cí) in Chinese. Measure Words are used along with a number in order to express the quantity of a noun (or sometimes action). The term "measure word" is sometimes referred to as a "classifier", used to denote the grouping of the words being counted. Whichever one you choose to call it, it's useful to ask if unsure, "What is (noun's) measure word?" Two ways to do this are:

(noun) 的單位是什麼?	(noun) de dān wèi shì shén me?
(noun) 的量詞是什麼?	(noun) de liàng cí shì shén me?

The majority of nouns have at least one specific measure word associated with them. According to some linguists, one way of grouping them is according to the 'descriptive quality' of what they're paired with. For instance, long, thin objects / animals often use the classifier 條 (tiáo, such as roads, cords, fish, snakes), objects with handles use 把 (bǎ, such as umbrellas, forks, or knives), and flat items use 張 (zhāng, sheets of paper, photos, tables, paper money, beds). The "catch all" measure word is 個 (ge), which, *in a pinch, can be used instead of the actual classifier if you've forgotten*. This word is extremely useful, as it's also just the standard measure word for many nouns.

Depending on which scholarly source you check, the number of official classifiers ranges from a few dozen to upwards of a few hundred. What's the good news in this? Well, there are only about two dozen that are frequently spoken, so in order to express yourself properly, you don't need to worry about a huge burden of extra vocabulary to memorize! Below is a table of the top 34 measure words, with the twenty most common in **bold** (of course this varies depending on the topics you commonly discuss).

Measure Word	pinyin	Qualities / Objects
1. 把	bǎ	Handled objects
2. 包	bāo	Bags
3. 杯	bēi	Cups
4. 本	běn	Books, notebooks, volumes, etc.
5. 部	bù	Cell phones, movies
6. 次	cì	Times (once, twice, etc.)
7. 朵	duǒ	For flowers, clustered items
8. 份	fèn	Sets of things
9. 個	ge	General measure word, use liberally!
10. 根	gēn	Long, rigid things, like sticks
11. 罐	guàn	Cans, tins of things
12. 家	jiā	Families, restaurants, businesses
13. 件	jiàn	Clothing, gifts
14. 間	jiān	Houses, rooms
15. 顆	kē	Round, balled objects
16. 棵	kē	Trees
17. 口	kǒu	Mouths, mouths to feed, openings
18. 塊	kuài	Chunk / piece of something, soap, cloth, bread
19. 輛	liàng	Cars, trucks
20. 盤	pán	Plates
21. 匹	pǐ	Horses
22. 片	piàn	Slices of things
23. 瓶	píng	Bottles
24. 首	shǒu	Songs or poems
25. 雙	shuāng	Pairs of things
26. 台	tái	Machines, machinery
27. 條	tiáo	Long, thin objects / animals (ex. ropes, snakes), roads, pants
28. 頭	tóu	Large animals (cows, sheep, elephants)
29. 碗	wǎn	Bowls
30. 位	wèi	People (politely)
31. 張	zhāng	Flat objects: papers, tables, etc.
32. 隻	zhī	Animals (dogs, cats, rats, etc.), hands, feet
33. 支	zhī	Pens, pencils, cigarettes
34. 座	zuò	Large buildings, mountains

Keep in mind, there is some variance with nouns and classifiers: the same noun can be paired with different classifiers in different contexts. For instance:

One grape / a grape.	一顆葡萄	yì **kē** pú táo
A bunch of grapes.	一串葡萄	yí **chuàn** pú táo
One horse / a horse.	一匹馬	yì **pǐ** mǎ
A herd of horses.	一群馬	yì **qún** mǎ

*see "Chinese Tone Crash Course" section, below, for explanation of tone variances.

LANGUAGE TIPS: Measure Words!

Below are some of the "rules" for proper usage of measure words with nouns. Examples are given below so you can compare and contrast the placement of the nouns and their respective measure words. **Measure words** are used after numbers or demonstrative pronouns:

Five mountains.	五座山	wǔ zuò shān
This mountain.	這座山	zhè zuò shān
Those three mountains.	那三座山	nà sān zuò shān

Sometimes, measure words can be doubled (reduplicated) after the number "one" 一 (yī) to indicate "every".

| Every mountain. | 一座座山 | yí zuò zuò shān |

"HALF" & "MORE THAN" / 半 & 多

The word 半 (bàn) means "half", and if it's added **before** a measure word, it means "half of" something. If it's added **after** a measure word, it means "-- and a half". The word 多 (duō) added after a number and before the measure word means "more than (the given number)". Here are some examples:

Half a cup of coffee.	半杯咖啡	**bàn bēi** kā fēi
A cup and a half of coffee.	一杯半咖啡	yì **bēi bàn** kā fēi
More than 20 cups of coffee.	二十多杯咖啡	èr shí **duō bēi** kā fēi

Summary Notes and Tips!

- **Of important note: singular / plural Chinese nouns are indicated in a different way than in English. To achieve this, generally a suffix is added to express "more than one" of something.** The good news? That makes the grammar relatively simple!

- **Also of vital note: Measure words / Classifiers are a staple component of Chinese speaking! This means learning the correct "measure word" that goes along with each noun.** More things to memorize….so what's the good news? Well, the most common measure words repeat, and there are certain "themes" for associating a certain classifier with a type of noun. When in doubt, the "catch all" measure word is 個 (ge).

- As you further your studies, you'll find that many Chinese Verbs are also used as Nouns, which helps with vocabulary expansion. Examples of this include:

Noun / Verb 名詞 / 動詞 míng cí / dòng cí	Chinese / 中文 / zhōng wén	Pinyin / 拼音 / pīn yīn
Love	愛	ài
Performance	表現	biǎo xiàn
Study	學習	xué xí
Wish	希望	xī wàng
Work	工作	gōng zuò

"Plurals" Reference Chart

Singular vs Plural		Plural noun forms don't change! Easy!
Demonstrative pronouns	些	Make "this" and "that" into "these" and "those": add the suffix 些 (xiē)
"All"	都	Shows "more than one" of something. (dōu)
"Every"	每	Used with "all" + MW to emphasize more than one noun. (měi)
"-men" suffix	們	Make singular personal pronouns plural: add the suffix 們 (men)
Possession	的	Adding 的 shows ownership / association. (de)

Pinyin Reference Chart

Initials	Finals	
Pinyin	Pinyin	Pinyin
b	a	ya,-ia
p	o	yo
m	e	ye,-ie
f		
d	ai	yao,-iao
t	ei	you,-iu
n	ao	yan, -ian
l	ou	yin,-in
g	an	yang,-iang
k	en	ying,-ing
h	ang	wa,-ua
j	en	wo,-uo
q	eng	wai,-uai
x	er	wei,-ui
zh(i)	yi,-i	wan,-uan
ch(i)	wu, -u	wen,-un
sh(i)	yu,-u/	wang,-uang
r(i)		weng,-ong
z(i)		yue,- üe
c(i)		yuan,- üan
s(i)		yun, - ün
		yong, -iong

Tone Reference Chart

Tone	Tone Marks / Pinyin	Description
1st tone	—	high level
2nd tone	´	high rising
3rd tone	ˇ	falling and rising
4th tone	`	falling (from high to low)
Neutral tone		no set pitch

Chinese Tone Crash Course

Mandarin has four main tones and one neutral tone (thus, five in total), as outlined in the above chart. Learn them well, as this is an absolutely vital component to speaking correct Chinese. A syllable with an incorrect tone can mean an entirely different word altogether.

1. The first tone is high and level, and your voice is kept even for the entire syllable when pronouncing it. Some students find it helpful to think of "singing" an even note while saying this tone.
2. The second rises up distinctly. English speakers associate this type of rise in pitch with asking a question, a tip which sometimes helps new learners.

3. The third tone drops slightly before rising again. Often confused with the second tone by new learners. Spend lots of time differentiating between the two.

4. The fourth tone drops sharply when spoken. To native English-speakers, this type of pronunciation is similar to when one gives a direct command. Its drop is quite clear and distinct.

5. The neutral tone is usually not shown on Mandarin tone charts because it doesn't really have a pitch. It's simply spoken quickly and relatively lightly, so it's somewhat more intuitive to English speakers. Syllables with a neutral tone have no tone marking in *pinyin*.

Crucial Tone Rules!

1. When two third tones are spoken in a row, the first one becomes a second tone! This rule never changes, and is found throughout the language.

2. When the negation word 不 (bù) precedes a fourth tone, 不 changes to second tone (bú). For example, "不對", meaning "not correct". This is very useful when you're negating verbs, so pay attention to this!

3. The word 一 (yī), means "one", and is first tone when spoken alone. However, it becomes a second tone when followed by a fourth tone. For example, "一件衣服" (yí jiàn yī fú), meaning "a piece of clothing". It becomes a fourth tone when followed by any other tone. An example of this is "一台車" (yì tái chē), meaning "a / one car".

Let's begin!

我們開始吧!

wǒ men kāi shǐ ba!

Lesson 1

第一課

dì yī kè

Airport

機場

jī chǎng

Airplane

飛機

fēi jī

Measure word	架 jià / 台 tái
Question	Did you see that giant airplane? 你有看到那架巨大的**飛機**嗎? nǐ yǒu kàn dào nà jià jù dà de **fēi jī** ma?
Answer	Yes, that's a giant airplane. 有,那是一台很大的**飛機**。 yǒu, nà shì yì tái hěn dà de fēi jī

Blanket

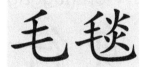

毛毯

máo tǎn

Measure word	件 jiàn
Question	Do you have an extra blanket? 你有多一件**毛毯**嗎? nǐ yǒu duō yí jiàn **máo tǎn** ma?
Answer	No, I only have this one. 沒有,我只有這件。 méi yǒu, wǒ zhǐ yǒu zhè jiàn

Boarding pass

登機證

dēng jī zhèng

Measure word	張 zhāng
Question	Did you get a boarding pass? 你拿到**登機證**了嗎? nǐ ná dào **dēng jī zhèng** le ma?
Answer	Yes, but why do I have two boarding passes? 有,但為什麼我有兩張**登機證**? yǒu, dàn wèi shé me wǒ yǒu liǎng zhāng **dēng jī zhèng**?

Carry-on (luggage)

隨身行李

suí shēn xíng lǐ

Measure word	件 jiàn
Question	Where's your carry-on? 你的**隨身行李**在哪裡? nǐ de **suí shēn xíng lǐ** zài nǎ lǐ?
Answer	I don't have carry-on this time. 我這次沒有**隨身行李**。 wǒ zhè cì méi yǒu **suí shēn xíng lǐ**

Cart

推車

tuī chē

Measure word	台 tái
Question	Can you get me a luggage cart? 你能幫我拿一台行李**推車**嗎？ nǐ néng bāng wǒ ná yì tái xíng lǐ **tuī chē** ma?
Answer	I don't see any carts here. 我這邊沒看到任何**推車**。 wǒ zhè biān méi kàn dào rèn hé **tuī chē**

Counter

櫃檯

guì tái

Measure word	個 ge
Question	At which counter should we check in? 我們應該在哪一個**櫃台**劃位？ wǒ men yīng gāi zài nǎ yí ge **guì tái** huà wèi?
Answer	That one in the front. 前面那個。 qián miàn nà ge

Flight attendant

空服員

kōng fú yuán

Measure word	位 wèi
Question	Do you think being a flight attendant is easy? 你覺得當一位**空服員**簡單嗎? nǐ jué de dāng yí wèi **kōng fú yuán** jiǎn dān ma?
Answer	No, not easy at all. 不, 一點也不簡單。 bù, yì diǎn yě bù jiǎn dān

Gate

登機門

dēng jī mén

Measure word	個 ge
Question	Did we miss our gate? 我們錯過我們的**登機門**了嗎? wǒ men cuò guò wǒ men de **dēng jī mén** le ma?
Answer	No, our gate is right here. 沒有, 我們的**登機門**就在這。 méi yǒu, wǒ men de **dēng jī mén** jiù zài zhè

Luggage

行李

xíng lǐ

Measure word	件 jiàn
Question	How many pieces of luggage do you have? 你有幾件**行李**? nǐ yǒu jǐ jiàn **xíng lǐ**?
Answer	I have three. 我有三件。 wǒ yǒu sān jiàn

Passport

護照

hù zhào

Measure word	本 běn
Question	Why do you have four passports? 為什麼你有四本**護照**? wèi shé me nǐ yǒu sì běn **hù zhào**?
Answer	No, the other three are pamphlets. 不是, 其他三本是小冊子。 bú shì, qí tā sān běn shì xiǎo cè zi

Seat

座位

zuò wèi

Measure word	個 ge
Question	Is that seat available? 那個**座位**可以坐嗎？ nà ge **zuò wèi** kě yǐ zuò ma?
Answer	That seat is dirty. 那個**座位**很髒。 nà ge **zuò wèi** hěn zāng

Seat belt

安全帶

ān quán dài

Measure word	條 tiáo
Question	Do you see the seat belt next to you? 你看到你旁邊那條**安全帶**嗎？ nǐ kàn dào nǐ páng biān nà tiáo **ān quán dài** ma?
Answer	I don't see any seat belt. 我沒看到任何**安全帶**。 wǒ méi kàn dào rèn hé **ān quán dài**

Shuttle bus

接駁巴士

jiē bó bā shì

Measure word	台 tái
Question	Did you book a shuttle bus?
	你有預訂一台**接駁巴士**嗎？
	nǐ yǒu yù dìng yì tái **jiē bó bā shì** ma?
Answer	Yes, I booked it a long time ago.
	是的, 我很久前就訂了。
	shì de, wǒ hěn jiǔ qián jiù dìng le

Taxi

計程車

jì chéng chē

Measure word	台 tái
Question	What color is our taxi?
	我們的**計程車**是什麼顏色？
	wǒ men de **jì chéng chē** shì shén me yán sè?
Answer	Most taxis in this city are yellow.
	這個城市的**計程車**大部分是黃色。
	zhè ge chéng shì de **jì chéng chē** dà bù fèn shì huáng sè

Terminal

航廈

háng shà

Measure word	個 ge
Question	Which terminal do you need to go to? 你需要到哪個**航廈**？ nǐ xū yào dào nǎ ge **háng shà**?
Answer	I need to go to terminal two. 我要到第二**航廈**。 wǒ yào dào dì èr **háng shà**

Ticket

piào

Measure word	張 zhāng
Question	How many tickets did you buy? 你買幾張**票**？ nǐ mǎi jǐ zhāng **piào**?
Answer	Like you said, four tickets. 照你說的, 四張**票**。 zhào nǐ shuō de, sì zhāng **piào**

Visa

qiān zhèng

Measure word	張 zhāng
Question	Where's your visa? 你的簽證在哪？ nǐ de **qiān zhèng** zài nǎ?
Answer	I still haven't gotten a visa yet. 我還沒拿到簽證 wǒ hái méi ná dào **qiān zhèng**

Lesson 2

第二課

dì èr kè

Bathroom

浴室

yù shì

Bathtub

浴缸

yù gāng

Measure word	個 ge / 座 zuò
Question	When are you going to fix the bathtub? 你什麼時候要修**浴缸**? nǐ shén me shí hòu yào xiū **yù gāng**?
Answer	I think I need to buy a new one. 我想我需要買一個新的。 wǒ xiǎng wǒ xū yāo mǎi yí ge xīn de

Conditioner

潤髮乳

rùn fǎ rǔ

Measure word	瓶 píng
Question	Did you see the bottle of conditioner I just bought? 你有看到我新買的那瓶**潤髮乳**嗎? nǐ yǒu kàn dào wǒ xīn mǎi de nà píng **rùn fǎ rǔ** ma?
Answer	I think you forgot it at the store. 我想你把它留在商店裡。 wǒ xiǎng nǐ bǎ tā liú zài shāng diàn lǐ

Cotton swab

棉花棒

mián huā bàng

Measure word	支 zhī
Question	Can you pass me a cotton swab? 你可以拿一支**棉花棒**給我嗎? nǐ kěyǐ ná yì zhī **mián huā bàng** gěi wǒ ma?
Answer	Here, this is the last one. 拿去,這是最後一支。 ná qù, zhè shì zuì hòu yì zhī

Electric razor

電動刮鬍刀

diàn dòng guā hú dāo

Measure word	支 zhī / 台 tái
Question	Do you use an electric razor? 你用**電動刮鬍刀**嗎? nǐ yòng **diàn dòng guā hú dāo** ma?
Answer	I have one, but I've never used it. 我有一台,但我從沒用過。 wǒ yǒu yì tái, dàn wǒ cóng méi yòng guò

Faucet

水龍頭

shuǐ lóng tóu

Measure word	個 ge
Question	Do you know you forgot to turn off the faucet this morning? 你知道你今天早上忘記關**水龍頭**嗎？ nǐ zhī dào nǐ jīn tiān zǎo shàng wàng jì guān **shuǐ lóng tóu** ma?
Answer	I didn't know, sorry. 我不知道, 抱歉。 wǒ bù zhī dào, bào qiàn

Hairdryer

吹風機

chuī fēng jī

Measure word	台 tái
Question	Did you use my hairdryer? 你用了我的**吹風機**嗎？ nǐ yòng le wǒ de **chuī fēng jī** ma?
Answer	I'd never use your rainbow-colored hairdryer. 我才不會用你那台彩虹色**吹風機**。 wǒ cái bú huì yòng nǐ nà tái cǎi hóng sè **chuī fēng jī**

Mirror

jìng zi

Measure word	面 miàn
Question	Who broke the mirror in the living room? 誰打破客廳裡那面**鏡子**? shuí dǎ pò kè tīng lǐ nà miàn **jìng zi**?
Answer	It fell off from the wall last night. 昨晚, 它從牆上掉下來。 zuó wǎn, tā cóng qiáng shàng diào xià lái

Perfume

xiāng shuǐ

Measure word	瓶 píng
Question	Where did you buy this bottle of perfume? 你在哪買這瓶**香水**的? nǐ zài nǎ mǎi zhè píng **xiāng shuǐ** de
Answer	It was a gift from my ex-boyfriend. 我前男友送的。 wǒ qián nán yǒu sòng de

Razor

刮鬍刀

guā hú dāo

Measure word	支 zhī
Question	Did you use my razor? 你用了我的**刮鬍刀**嗎? nǐ yòng le wǒ de **guā hú dāo** ma?
Answer	I'm not sure. Which one is yours? 我不確定。哪一支是你的? wǒ bú què dìng. nǎ yì zhī shì nǐ de?

Shampoo

洗髮精

xǐ fǎ jīng

Measure word	瓶 píng
Question	Why do you like this bottle of shampoo? 你為什麼喜歡這瓶**洗髮精**? nǐ wèi shéme xǐ huān zhè píng **xǐ fǎ jīng**?
Answer	I like the big bottle and the cheap price. 我喜歡它大瓶又便宜。 wǒ xǐ huān tā dà píng yòu pián yí

Shower head

蓮蓬頭

lián peng tóu

Measure word	個 ge
Question	Why is the shower head so dirty? 為什麼這個蓮蓬頭這麼髒? wèi shé me zhè ge **lián peng tóu** zhè me zāng?
Answer	Because you never clean it! 因為你從來沒清洗啊! yīn wèi nǐ cóng lái méi qīng xǐ a

Soap

肥皂

féi zào

Measure word	塊 kuài
Question	What do you like about this soap? 你喜歡這塊肥皂的什麼? nǐ xǐ huān zhè kuài **féi zào** de shén me?
Answer	I like the scent and the ingredients. 我喜歡它的味道和成份。 wǒ xǐ huān tā de wèi dào hàn chéng fèn

Tile

磁磚

cí zhuān

Measure word	片 piàn
Question	Did you use tiles for your floor? 你的地板是用**磁磚**嗎? nǐ de dì bǎn shì yòng **cí zhuān** ma?
Answer	Yes, but I broke one. 沒錯... 但我打破一片。 méi cuò... dàn wǒ dǎ pò yí piàn

Tissue

衛生紙

wèi shēng zhǐ

Measure word	張 zhāng
Question	Can you pass me a tissue? 你可以拿張**衛生紙**給我嗎? nǐ kě yǐ ná zhāng **wèi shēng zhǐ** gěi wǒ ma?
Answer	Actually, I think we're out of tissues. 其實,我們沒有**衛生紙**了。 qí shí, wǒ men méi yǒu **wèi shēng zhǐ** le

Tooth brush

牙刷

yá shuā

Measure word	支 zhī
Question	Where can I buy a new tooth brush? 我在哪裡可以買支新**牙刷**? wǒ zài nǎ lǐ kě yǐ mǎi zhī xīn **yá shuā**?
Answer	You could try a pharmacy. 你可以到藥局試試。 nǐ kě yǐ dào yào jú shì shì

Toothpaste

牙膏

yá gāo

Measure word	條 tiáo
Question	Do we need to buy toothpaste? 我們需要買**牙膏**嗎? wǒ men xū yào mǎi **yá gāo** ma?
Answer	No, we still have a new toothpaste at home. 不用,我們還有一條新的**牙膏**在家。 bù yòng, wǒ men hái yǒu yì tiáo xīn de **yá gāo** zài jiā.

Towel

毛巾

máo jīn

Measure word	條 tiáo
Question	How many towels do you have? 你有幾條**毛巾**? nǐ yǒu jǐ tiáo **máo jīn**?
Answer	I have one, but I need to buy more. 一條, 但我需要多買一些。 yì tiáo, dàn wǒ xū yào duō mǎi yì xiē

Lesson 3

第三課

dì sān kè

Farm Animals

農場動物

nóng chǎng dòng wù

Cat

貓

māo

Measure word	隻 zhī
Question	Do you like cats? 你喜歡貓嗎? nǐ xǐ huān **māo** ma?
Answer	Yes, I have two cats at home actually. 喜歡, 我其實有兩隻貓在家。 xǐ huān, wǒ qí shí yǒu liǎng zhī **māo** zài jiā

Chicken

雞

jī

Measure word	隻 zhī
Question	Do you like watching chicken fights? 你喜歡看雞打架嗎? nǐ xǐ huān kàn **jī** dǎ jià ma?
Answer	No, that's too cruel for the chickens. 不喜歡, 那對雞來說太殘忍了。 bù xǐ huān, nà duì **jī** lái shuō tài cán rěn le

Cow

乳牛

rǔ niú

Quantifier	頭 tóu
Question	Have you counted how many cows are at the farm? 你曾算過農場上有幾頭**乳牛**嗎? nǐ céng suàn guò nóng chǎng shàng yǒu jǐ tóu **rǔ niú** ma?
Answer	No, there are too many cows. 沒有, 太多**乳牛**了。 méi yǒu, tài duō **rǔ niú** le

Dog

狗

gǒu

Measure word	條 tiáo / 隻 zhī
Question	Is that dog injured? 那隻**狗**受傷了嗎? nà zhī **gǒu** shòu shāng le ma?
Answer	It looks like both of those dogs are hurt. 看起來好像兩隻**狗**都受傷了。 kàn qǐ lái hǎo xiàng liǎng zhī **gǒu** dōu shòu shāng le

Donkey

驢子

lǘ zi

Measure word	頭 tóu
Question	When did you get that donkey? 你什麼時候有那頭**驢子**？ nǐ shén me shí hòu yǒu nà tóu **lǘ zi**?
Answer	I've had that donkey since I was a kid. 從我小時候就有那頭**驢子**了。 cóng wǒ xiǎo shí hòu jiù yǒu nà tóu **lǘ zi** le

Duck

鴨子

yā zi

Measure word	隻 zhī
Question	How many ducks are over there? 那邊有幾隻**鴨子**？ nà biān yǒu jǐ zhī **yā zi**?
Answer	I saw three ducks. 我看到三隻**鴨子**。 wǒ kàn dào sān zhī **yā zi**

Goat

山羊

shān yáng

Measure word	隻 zhī / 頭 tóu
Question	Do you see the goat climbing on the mountain? 你看到那隻**山羊**爬山嗎? nǐ kàn dào nà zhī **shān yáng** pá shān ma?
Answer	Yes, that goat climbed really high. 有,那隻**山羊**爬很高。 yǒu, nà zhī **shān yáng** pá hěn gāo

Pig

豬

zhū

Measure word	隻 zhī / 頭 tóu
Question	Would you buy a mini pig as a pet? 你會買一隻迷你**豬**當寵物嗎? nǐ huì mǎi yì zhī mí nǐ **zhū** dāng chǒng wù ma?
Answer	No, they always turn into giant pigs. 不會,他們總是變成大**豬**。 bú huì, tā men zǒng shì biàn chéng dà **zhū**

Rabbit

tù zi

Measure word	隻 zhī
Question	How high can your rabbit jump? 你那隻**兔子**能跳多高？ nǐ nà zhī **tù zi** néng tiào duō gāo?
Answer	My rabbit is lazy, he has never jumped. 我的**兔子**很懶，他從沒跳過。 wǒ de tù zi hěn lǎn, tā cóng méi tiào guò

Rat

lǎo shǔ

Measure word	隻 zhī
Question	Did you see a rat running by? 你有看到一隻**老鼠**跑過去嗎？ nǐ yǒu kàn dào yì zhī **lǎo shǔ** pǎo guò qù ma?
Answer	Where?! I'm afraid of rats the most. 哪裡？！我最怕**老鼠**了。 nǎ lǐ ?! wǒ zuì pà **lǎo shǔ** le

Sheep

綿羊

mián yáng

Measure word	隻 zhī
Question	Why is that sheep so stinky? 為什麼那隻羊這麼臭？ wèi shé me nà zhī **yáng** zhè me chòu?
Answer	Its owner hasn't cleaned it for a while. 它的主人好一陣子沒清理它了。 tā de zhǔ rén hǎo yí zhèn zi méi qīng lǐ tā le

Turkey

火雞

huǒ jī

Measure word	隻 zhī
Question	Did you see two turkeys crossing the road? 你剛有看到兩隻火雞過馬路嗎？ nǐ gāng yǒu kàn dào liǎng zhī **huǒ jī** guò mǎ lù ma?
Answer	hm, no..., I didn't see any turkeys. 嗯,沒有...,我沒看到任何火雞。 en, méi yǒu..., wǒ méi kàn dào rèn hé **huǒ jī**

Lesson 4

第四課

dì sì kè

Fruits

水果

shuǐ guǒ

Apple

蘋果

píng guǒ

Measure word	顆 kē
Question	I have an apple; do you want it? 我有一顆**蘋果**，你要嗎？ wǒ yǒu yì kē **píng guǒ**, nǐ yào ma?
Answer	No, thanks. I just ate an apple. 不用，謝謝。我才吃一顆**蘋果**。 bú yòng, xiè xie. wǒ cái chī yì kē **píng guǒ**

Avocado

酪梨

luò lí

Measure word	顆 kē
Question	How many avocados do you need to make avocado toast? 你需要幾顆**酪梨**做**酪梨**吐司？ nǐ xū yào jǐ kē **luò lí** zuò **luò lí** tǔ sī?
Answer	I usually use half an avocado. 我通常用半顆**酪梨**。 wǒ tōng cháng yòng bàn kē **luò lí**

Banana

香蕉

xiāng jiāo

Measure word	根 gēn / 串 chuàn
Question	Why did you buy this big bunch of bananas?
	你為什麼買這一大串香蕉?
	nǐ wèi shé me mǎi zhè yí dà chuàn **xiāng jiāo**?
Answer	I need one banana for my daily smoothie.
	我每天的奶昔都需要一根香蕉。
	wǒ měi tiān de nǎi xí dōu xū yào yì gēn xiāng jiāo

Cherry

櫻桃

yīng táo

Measure word	顆 kē
Question	How many cherries are in your cake?
	你的蛋糕裡有幾顆櫻桃?
	nǐ de dàn gāo lǐ yǒu jǐ kē **yīng táo**
Answer	Only two...It's a scam!
	只有兩顆...真是詐騙!
	zhǐ yǒu liǎng kē... zhēn shi zhà piàn!

Coconut

椰子

yé zi

Measure word	顆 kē
Question	Can you pick a coconut from the tree for me? 你可以從樹上摘一顆**椰子**給我嗎？ nǐ kě yǐ cóng shù shàng zhāi yì kē **yé zi** gěi wǒ ma?
Answer	Do you need one or two coconuts? 你需要一顆還是兩顆**椰子**？ nǐ xū yào yì kē hái shì liǎng kē **yé zi**?

Grapefruit

葡萄柚

pú táo yòu

Measure word	顆 kē
Question	Is your grapefruit juicy? 你那顆**葡萄柚**多汁嗎？ nǐ nà kē **pú táo yòu** duō zhī ma?
Answer	Yes, but this one is also really sour. 多汁, 但這顆也很酸。 duō zhī, dàn zhè kē yě hěn suān.

Grapes

葡萄

pú táo

Measure word	顆 kē / 串 chuàn
Question	Do you want to buy a bunch of grapes? 你要買一串**葡萄**嗎？ nǐ yào mǎi yí chuàn **pú táo** ma?
Answer	No, I don't like grapes. 不用, 我不喜歡**葡萄**。 bú yòng, wǒ bù xǐ huān **pú táo**

Lemon

檸檬

níng méng

Measure word	顆 kē
Question	Can I borrow a lemon from you? 我可以跟你借一顆**檸檬**嗎？ wǒ kě yǐ gēn nǐ jiè yì kē **níng méng** ma?
Answer	I'll just *give* you a lemon, it's nothing. 我直接給你一顆**檸檬**就好, 小事。 wǒ zhí jiē gěi nǐ yì kē **níng méng** jiù hǎo, xiǎo shì

Orange

柳橙

liǔ chéng

Measure word	顆 kē
Question	Do you bring an orange with you every day?! 你每天都帶一顆**柳橙**嗎？！ nǐ měi tiān dū dài yì kē **liǔ chéng** ma?!
Answer	Yeah, I really like eating oranges. 對啊，我真的很喜歡吃**柳橙**。 duì a, wǒ zhēn de hěn xǐ huān chī **liǔ chéng**

Peach

水蜜桃

shuǐ mì táo

Measure word	顆 kē
Question	Why are peaches so expensive this year? 為什麼**水蜜桃**今年這麼貴？ wèi shé me **shuǐ mì táo** jīn nián zhè me guì?
Answer	Yeah, one peach costs a fortune. 對啊，一顆**水蜜桃**要花很多錢。 duì a, yì kē **shuǐ mì táo** yào huā hěn duō qián

Pear

lí zi

Measure word	顆 kē
Question	Have you ever made a pear cake? 你做過**梨子**蛋糕嗎？ nǐ zuò guò **lí zi** dàn gāo ma?
Answer	I've never heard of it. I'd rather just eat a pear. 從沒聽過。我寧願吃一顆**梨子**。 cóng méi tīng guò. wǒ níng yuàn chī yì kē **lí zi**

Pineapple

fèng lí

Measure word	顆 kē
Question	Do you know how to cut pineapple efficiently? 你知道如何有效率的切**鳳梨**嗎？ nǐ zhī dào rú hé yǒu xiào lǜ de qiē **fèng lí** ma?
Answer	I just got this one, so you can teach me. 我剛拿到這顆，所以你可以教我。 wǒ gāng ná dào zhè kē, suǒ yǐ nǐ kě yǐ jiāo wǒ

Strawberry

草莓

cǎo méi

Measure word	顆 kē
Question	How many strawberries are in the box? 盒子裡有幾顆**草莓**? hé zi lǐ yǒu jǐ kē **cǎo méi**
Answer	I think there are fifteen strawberries inside. 我想裡面有十五顆**草莓**。 wǒ xiǎng lǐ miàn yǒu shí wǔ kē **cǎo méi**

Tangerine

橘子

jú zi

Measure word	顆 kē
Question	Did you see that ugly tangerine? 你有看到那顆很醜的**橘子**嗎? nǐ yǒu kàn dào nà kē hěn chǒu de **jú zi** ma?
Answer	Shh...you'll hurt the ugly tangerine's feelings. 噓...你會傷到那顆醜**橘子**的心。 xū... nǐ huì shāng dào nà kē chǒu **jú zi** de xīn

Watermelon

xī guā

Measure word	顆 kē
Question	Do you know how long it takes to grow a watermelon? 你知道種一顆**西瓜**要多久嗎？ nǐ zhī dào zhòng yì kē **xī guā** yào duō jiǔ ma?
Answer	No, I only know how long it takes me to eat a watermelon. 不知道，我只知道我吃一顆**西瓜**要多久。 bù zhī dào, wǒ zhǐ zhī dào wǒ chī yì kē **xī guā** yào duō jiǔ

Lesson 5

第五課

dì wǔ kè

Kitchen

廚房

chú fáng

Blender

果汁機

guǒ zhī jī

Measure word	台 tái
Question	Why do you have so many blenders? 為什麼你有這麼多台**果汁機**? Wèi shé me nǐ yǒu zhè me duō tái **guǒ zhī jī**
Answer	Some of them are broken. 有幾台是壞掉的。 Yǒu jǐ tái shì huài diào de

Bottle opener

開瓶器

kāi píng qì

Measure word	支 zhī
Question	Have you seen my bottle opener? 你有看到我那支**開瓶器**嗎? nǐ yǒu kàn dào wǒ nà zhī **kāi píng qì** ma?
Answer	Which one? You have a few, don't you? 哪一支? 你有好幾支, 不是嗎? nǎ yí zhī? nǐ yǒu hǎo jǐ zhī, bú shì ma?

Bowl

wǎn

Measure word	個 ge
Question	Don't you think this bowl is pretty? 你不覺得這個**碗**很漂亮嗎？ nǐ bù jué de zhè ge **wǎn** hěn piào liang ma?
Answer	I think that bowl over there is prettier. 我認為那邊的**碗**更漂亮。 wǒ rèn wéi nà biān de wǎn gèng piào liang

Chair

yǐ zi

Measure word	張 zhāng / 把 bǎ
Question	Is that chair made of cardboard? 那張**椅子**是紙板做成的嗎？ nà zhāng **yǐ zi** shì zhǐ bǎn zuò chéng de ma
Answer	It looks that way. The quality looks poor. 看起來是。品質看起來不好。 kàn qǐ lái shì. pǐn zhí kàn qǐ lái bù hǎo

Chopsticks

筷 子

kuài zi

Measure word	雙　shuāng
Question	Do you need a pair of chopsticks for dinner? 你需要一雙筷子吃晚餐嗎？ nǐ xū yào yì shuāng **kuài zi** chī wǎn cān ma?
Answer	I'm okay with a spoon, thanks. 我用湯匙就好, 謝謝。 wǒ yòng tāng chí jiù hǎo, xiè xie

Coffee maker

咖啡機

kā fēi jī

Measure word	台　tái
Question	How should I use the coffee machine? 我該如何用這台咖啡機？ wǒ gāi rú hé yòng zhè tái **kā fēi jī**
Answer	It's a bit complicated, I'll help you. 這有點複雜, 我幫你。 zhè yǒu diǎn fù zá, wǒ bāng nǐ

Cup

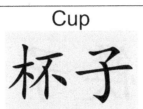

bēi zi

Measure word	個 ge
Question	Can I use this cup? 我可以用這個**杯子**嗎？ wǒ kě yǐ yòng zhè ge **bēi zi** ma
Answer	Of course, as long as it's clean. 當然可以, 只要它是乾淨的。 dāng rán kě yǐ, zhǐ yào tā shì gān jìng de

Fork

chā zi

Measure word	把 bǎ
Question	Who dropped a fork under the table? 誰掉了一把**叉子**在桌下？ shuí diào le yì bǎ **chā zi** zài zhuō xià?
Answer	Where? I don't see any forks under the table. 哪裡？我沒看到任何**叉子**在桌下。 nǎ lǐ? wǒ méi kàn dào rèn hé **chā zi** zài zhuō xià

Glass

玻璃杯

bō lí bēi

Measure word	個 ge
Question	What did you give me this glass for? 你為什麼給我這個**玻璃杯**？ nǐ wèi shé me gěi wǒ zhè ge **bō lí bēi**?
Answer	It's for your beer. 給你喝啤酒用的。 gěi nǐ hē pí jiǔ yòng de

Knife

刀子

dāo zi

Measure word	把 bǎ
Question	How many knives are in this set? 這個刀具有幾把**刀子**？ zhè ge dāo jù yǒu jǐ bǎ **dāo zi**
Answer	There are ten knives in different sizes. 十把不同尺寸的**刀子**。 shí bǎ bù tóng chǐ cùn de **dāo zi**

Lid

蓋子

gài zi

Measure word	個 ge
Question	Can you put a lid on the pan? 你可以在煎鍋上放一個**蓋子**嗎? nǐ kě yǐ zài jiān guō shàng fàng yí ge **gài zi** ma?
Answer	I can't find any lids! 我找不到任何**蓋子**。 wǒ zhǎo bú dào rèn hé **gài zi**

Napkin

餐巾紙

cān jīn zhǐ

Measure word	張 zhāng
Question	Can you pass me a napkin? 你可以拿一張**餐巾紙**給我嗎? nǐ kě yǐ ná yì zhāng **cān jīn zhǐ** gěi wǒ ma?
Answer	You're messy, I'll give you two! 你好髒, 我給你兩張好了! nǐ hǎo zāng, wǒ gěi nǐ liǎng zhāng hǎo le!

Oven

烤箱

kǎo xiāng

Measure word	台 tái
Question	What are you baking in the oven? 你那台**烤箱**在烤什麼？ nǐ nà tái **kǎo xiāng** zài kǎo shén me?
Answer	I decided to bake an apple pie. 我決定烤一個蘋果派。 wǒ jué dìng kǎo yí ge píng guǒ pài

Plate

盤子

pán zi

Measure word	個 ge
Question	Why there are so many plates in the sink? 為什麼水槽裡有這麼多個**盤子**？ Wèi shé me shuǐ cáo lǐ yǒu zhè me duō ge **pán zi**?
Answer	I was sick, so I haven't washed dishes for days. 我生病了，所以好幾天沒洗碗。 wǒ shēng bìng le, suǒ yǐ hǎo jǐ tiān méi xǐ wǎn

Pot

鍋子

guō zi

Measure word	口 kǒu / 個 ge
Question	What are you going to use this pot for? 你要用這個**鍋子**做什麼？ nǐ yào yòng zhè ge **guō zi** zuò shén me?
Answer	This pot is perfect for making soup. 這個**鍋子**很適合煮湯。 zhè ge **guō zi** hěn shì hé zhǔ tāng

Skillet

煎鍋

jiān guō

Measure word	個 ge
Question	Did you buy a new skillet? 你買了一個新的**煎鍋**嗎？ nǐ mǎi le yī gè xīn de **jiān guō** ma?
Answer	Actually, I got three skillets. 其實，我買了三個**煎鍋**。 qí shí, wǒ mǎi le sān ge **jiān guō**

Sponge

海綿

hǎi mián

Measure word	塊 kuài
Question	Where did you put the sponge? 你把**海綿**放哪裡了？ nǐ bǎ **hǎi mián** fàng nǎ lǐ le?
Answer	There's a sponge next to the sink. 水槽旁邊有一塊**海綿**。 shuǐ cáo páng biān yǒu yí kuài **hǎi mián**

Spoon

湯匙

tāng chí

Measure word	支 zhī
Question	Do you need a spoon? 你需要一支**湯匙**嗎？ nǐ xū yào yì zhī **tāng chí** ma?
Answer	Yes, I need to stir my tea. 好，我需要攪拌我的茶。 hǎo, wǒ xū yào jiǎo bàn wǒ de chá

Table

桌子

zhuō zi

Measure word	張 zhāng
Question	When did get this table? 你什麼時候有這張**桌子**? nǐ shén me shí hòu yǒu zhè zhāng **zhuō zi**?
Answer	I got it on sale last year. 我去年折扣的時候買的。 wǒ qù nián zhé kòu de shí hòu mǎi de

Toaster

kǎo miàn bāo jī

Measure word	台 tái
Question	When did you clean the toaster? 你什麼時候清理這台烤麵包機? nǐ shén me shí hòu qīng lǐ zhè tái **kǎo miàn bāo jī**?
Answer	I cleaned it yesterday when I came home. 我昨天回家時清理的。 wǒ zuó tiān huí jiā shí qīng lǐ de

Lesson 6

第六課

dì liù kè

Office

辦公室

bàn gōng shì

Pen

筆

bǐ

Measure word	隻 zhī
Question	Can I borrow a pen? 我可以跟你借隻筆嗎? wǒ kě yǐ gēn nǐ jiè zhī **bǐ** ma?
Answer	What kind of pen do you need? 你需要哪一種筆? nǐ xū yào nǎ yì zhǒng **bǐ**?

Calculator

計算機

jì suàn jī

Measure word	台 tái
Question	Is your calculator out of power? 你這台計算機沒電了嗎? nǐ zhè tái **jì suàn jī** méi diàn le ma?
Answer	No way! I just changed the battery. 不可能, 我才換了電池。 bù kě néng, wǒ cái huàn le diàn chí

Computer

電腦

diàn nǎo

Measure word	台 tái
Question	How many computers do you have? 你有幾台電腦? nǐ yǒu jǐ tái **diàn nǎo**?
Answer	I can only afford one computer. 我只付得起一台電腦。 wǒ zhǐ fù de qǐ yì tái **diàn nǎo**

Copy machine

影印機

yǐng yìn jī

Measure word	台 tái
Question	Do you know how to use this copy machine? 你知道怎麼使用這台影印機嗎? nǐ zhī dào zěn me shǐ yòng zhè tái **yǐng yìn jī** ma?
Answer	Just press this button. 按這個按鈕就好。 àn zhè ge àn niǔ jiù hǎo

Correction fluid

修正液

xiū zhèng yì

Measure word	瓶 píng
Question	Do you have correction fluid? 你有一瓶**修正液**嗎？ nǐ yǒu yì píng **xiū zhèng yì** ma?
Answer	No, I only have an eraser. 沒有，我只有橡皮擦。 méi yǒu, wǒ zhǐ yǒu xiàng pí cā

Extension cord

延長線

yán cháng xiàn

Measure word	條 tiáo
Question	Should we get an extension cord? 我們應該買條**延長線**嗎？ wǒ men yīng gāi mǎi tiáo **yán cháng xiàn** ma?
Answer	No, we don't need an extension cord. 不用，我們不需要**延長線**。 bú yòng, wǒ men bù xū yào **yán cháng xiàn**

Folder

資料夾

zī liào jiá

Measure word	個 ge
Question	Do you like this folder? 你喜歡這個**資料夾**嗎? nǐ xǐ huān zhè ge **zī liào jiá** ma?
Answer	Yeah, they're very useful. 喜歡, 它們很有用。 xǐ huān, tā men hěn yǒu yòng

Glue

膠水

jiāo shuǐ

Measure word	瓶 píng
Question	Where can I buy a bottle of glue? 我在哪裡可以買到一瓶**膠水**? wǒ zài nǎ lǐ kě yǐ mǎi dào yì píng **jiāo shuǐ**?
Answer	The stationery store nearby sells it. 附近的文具店有賣。 fù jìn de wén jù diàn yǒu mài

Highlighter

螢光筆

yíng guāng bǐ

Measure word	隻 zhī
Question	Which highlighter do you like? 你喜歡哪隻**螢光筆**？ nǐ xǐ huān nǎ zhī **yíng guāng bǐ**?
Answer	I like the pink highlighter. 我喜歡粉紅色的**螢光筆**。 wǒ xǐ huān fěn hóng sè de **yíng guāng bǐ**

Keyboard

鍵盤

jiàn pán

Measure word	個 ge
Question	Is your keyboard wireless? 你那個**鍵盤**是無線的嗎？ nǐ nà ge **jiàn pán** shì wú xiàn de ma?
Answer	No, this keyboard is quite old 不是,這個**鍵盤**很舊了 bú shì, zhè ge **jiàn pán** hěn jiù le

Letter

xìn

Measure word	封 fēng
Question	Is this your letter? 這封是你的信嗎? zhè fēng shì nǐ de xìn ma?
Answer	No, that's my neighbor's. 不是, 那是我鄰居的 。 bú shì, nà shì wǒ lín jū de

Light / lamp

dēng

Measure word	盞 zhǎn / 台 tái
Question	When did you buy this light? 你什麼時候買這台燈的? nǐ shén me shí hòu mǎi zhè tái **dēng** de
Answer	I've had that lamp for over ten years. 我有這台燈超過十年了 。 wǒ yǒu zhè tái **dēng** chāo guò shí nián le

Marker

馬克筆

mǎ kè bǐ

Measure word	隻 zhī
Question	How many markers do you have? 你有幾隻馬克筆? nǐ yǒu jǐ zhī **mǎ kè bǐ**
Answer	I have six markers for the presentation. 我為報告準備六隻馬克筆。 wǒ wèi bào gào zhǔn bèi liù zhī **mǎ kè bǐ**

Notebook

筆記本

bǐ jì běn

Measure word	本 běn
Question	Why do you need a notebook? 為什麼你需要一本筆記本? wèi shé me nǐ xū yào yì běn **bǐ jì běn**?
Answer	I like to write down ideas in a notebook. 我喜歡把想法寫在筆記本上。 wǒ xǐ huān bǎ xiǎng fǎ xiě zài **bǐ jì běn** shàng

Paper

紙

zhǐ

Measure word	張 zhāng
Question	Do you have a sheet of paper? 你有一張紙嗎? nǐ yǒu yì zhāng **zhǐ** ma?
Answer	I only have pink paper; do you want it? 我只有粉紅色的紙。你要嗎? wǒ zhǐ yǒu fěn hóng sè de **zhǐ**. nǐ yào ma?

Paper clip

迴紋針

huí wén zhēn

Measure word	個 ge
Question	Can I take a few paper clips? 我可以拿幾個迴紋針嗎? wǒ kě yǐ ná jǐ ge huí wén zhēn ma?
Answer	This is my last one, sorry. 這是我最後一個, 抱歉。 zhè shì wǒ zuì hòu yí ge, bào qiàn

Phone

電話

diàn huà

Measure word	台 tái
Question	Did you install a new phone?
	你裝了一台新**電話**嗎?
	nǐ zhuāng le yì tái xīn **diàn huà** ma?
Answer	Yeah, the last one was broken.
	對, 上一台壞掉了。
	duì, shàng yì tái huài diào le

Post-it

便利貼

biàn lì tiē

Measure word	張 zhāng
Question	Why do you have a post-it on your back?
	為什麼你有張**便利貼**在你背上?
	wèi shé me nǐ yǒu zhāng **biàn lì tiē** zài nǐ bèi shàng?
Answer	Oh, it must be a prank from someone.
	喔, 一定是某人的惡作劇。
	ō, yí dìng shì mǒu rén de è zuò jù

Rubber band

橡皮筋

xiàng pí jīn

Measure word	條 tiáo
Question	Can you wrap the cards with a rubber band?
	你可以用條**橡皮筋**綑這些卡嗎？
	nǐ kě yǐ yòng tiáo **xiàng pí jīn** kǔn zhè xiē kǎ ma?
Answer	Yeah, let me find a rubber band.
	可以, 讓我找條**橡皮筋**。
	kě yǐ, ràng wǒ zhǎo tiáo **xiàng pí jīn**.

Stamp / seal

印章

yìn zhāng

Measure word	個 ge
Question	Do you need the boss's stamp on the contract?
	你的合約上需要老闆的**章**嗎？
	nǐ de hé yuē shàng xū yào lǎo bǎn de **zhāng** ma?
Answer	Yes, without a stamp, it's not legal.
	對, 沒有**章**就不合法。
	duì, méi yǒu **zhāng** jiù bù hé fǎ

Stapler

釘書機

dìng shū jī

Measure word	個 ge
Question	Whose stapler is that? 那個是誰的釘書機？ nà ge shì shuí de **dìng shū jī**?
Answer	That's the new stapler I bought. 那是我買的新釘書機。 nà shì wǒ mǎi de xīn **dìng shū jī**

Tape

膠帶

jiāo dài

Measure word	捲 juǎn
Question	Can you give me a roll of tape? 你能給我一捲膠帶嗎？ nǐ néng gěi wǒ yì juǎn **jiāo dài** ma?
Answer	Sorry, I don't have any tape right now. 抱歉，我現在沒有任何膠帶。 bào qiàn, wǒ xiàn zài méi yǒu rèn hé **jiāo dài**

Lesson 7

第七課

dì qī kè

On the Street

在街上

zài jiē shàng

Apartment

公寓

gōng yù

Measure word	棟 dòng
Question	Do you own an apartment? 你擁有一棟**公寓**嗎? nǐ yǒng yǒu yí dòng **gōng yù** ma?
Answer	No, no way could I afford an apartment. 不, 我不可能付得起一棟**公寓**。 bù, wǒ bù kě néng fù de qǐ yí dòng **gōng yù**

Bicycle

腳踏車

jiǎo tà chē

Measure word	台 tái / 輛 liàng
Question	Whose bicycle is that? 那台**腳踏車**是誰的? nà tái **jiǎo tà chē** shì shuí de?
Answer	That bike belongs to my younger brother. 那台**腳踏車**是我弟弟的。 nà tái **jiǎo tà chē** shì wǒ dì di de

Bus stop

公車站

gōng chē zhàn

Measure word	個 ge
Question	Are we waiting at that bus stop? 我們是在那個**公車站**等嗎？ wǒ men shì zài nà ge **gōng chē zhàn** děng ma?
Answer	Yes, that's the bus stop. 沒錯，就是那個**公車站**。 méi cuò, jiù shì nà ge **gōng chē zhàn**

Car

汽車

qì chē

Measure word	部 bù / 輛 liàng / 台 tái
Question	Did you see that cool car? 你有看到那部/輛很酷的**汽車**嗎？ nǐ yǒu kàn dào nà bù / liàng hěn kù de **qì chē** ma?
Answer	No, I was just looking at another car. 沒有，我剛在看別台**汽車**。 méi yǒu, wǒ gāng zài kàn bié tái **qì chē**

Motorcycle

機車

jī chē

Measure word	輛 liàng
Question	Do you have a motorcycle? 你有一輛**機車**嗎？ nǐ yǒu yí liàng **jī chē** ma?
Answer	Yes, I do have a motorcycle. 是的，我有一輛**機車**。 shì de, wǒ yǒu yí liàng **jī chē**

Parking lot

停車場

tíng chē chǎng

Measure word	個 ge
Question	Should we park our car in that parking lot? 我們應該把車停在那個**停車場**嗎？ wǒ men yīng gāi bǎ chē tíng zài nà ge **tíng chē chǎng** ma?
Answer	Maybe not. The fee is too expensive. 應該不會，收費太貴了。 yīng gāi bú huì, shōu fèi tài guì le

Road

路

lù

Measure word	條 tiáo
Question	Do you know that road? 你知道那條路嗎? nǐ zhī dào nà tiáo lù ma?
Answer	Yes, my home is on that road. 知道, 我家就在那條路上。 zhī dào, wǒ jiā jiù zài nà tiáo lù shàng

Skyscraper

摩天大樓

mó tiān dà lóu

Measure word	棟 dòng / 幢 chuáng
Question	Did you see that skyscraper? 你有看到那棟/幢高樓大廈嗎? nǐ yǒu kàn dào nà dòng/chuáng **gāo lóu dà shà** ma?
Answer	Which one? 哪一棟/幢? nǎ yí dòng / chuáng?

Store

商店

shāng diàn

Measure word	間 jiān
Question	At which store did you buy that hat? 你在哪間**商店**買那頂帽子? nǐ zài nǎ jiān **shāng diàn** mǎi nà dǐng mào zi?
Answer	The one near my house. 我家附近那間。 wǒ jiā fù jìn nà jiān

Street

街

jiē

Measure word	條 tiáo
Question	Does he live on this street? 他住在這條**街**上嗎? tā zhù zài zhè tiáo **jiē** shàng ma?
Answer	I think so, or maybe it's the next street. 我想是啊, 或有可能是下一條**街**。 wǒ xiǎng shì a, huò yǒu kě néng shì xià yī tiáo **jiē**

Traffic light

紅綠燈

hóng lǜ dēng

Measure word	個 ge
Question	How did that traffic light get broken? 那個**紅綠燈**是怎麼壞掉的？ nà ge **hóng lǜ dēng** shì zěn me huài diào de?
Answer	Yesterday, it was hit by a car. 昨天被一台車撞到。 zuó tiān bèi yì tái chē zhuàng dào

Lesson 8

第八課

dì bā kè

Supermarket

超市

chāo shì

Bottled water

瓶裝水

píng zhuāng shuǐ

Measure word	瓶 píng
Question	Do you need a bottle of bottled water? 你需要一瓶**瓶裝水**嗎？ nǐ xū yào yì píng **píng zhuāng shuǐ** ma?
Answer	No, I brought water. It's greener. 不用，我有帶水。這對環境比較好。 bú yòng, wǒ yǒu dài shuǐ. zhè duì huán jìng bǐ jiào hǎo

Burger

漢堡

hàn bǎo

Measure word	個 ge
Question	How many burgers do you want? 你要幾個**漢堡**？ nǐ yào jǐ ge **hàn bǎo**?
Answer	Give me two burgers, please. I'm hungry. 請給我兩個**漢堡**，我很餓。 qǐng gěi wǒ liǎng ge **hàn bǎo,** wǒ hěn è

Cake

蛋糕

dàn gāo

Measure word	盒 hé / 塊 kuài
Question	I bought a box of cake, do you want some? 我買了一盒蛋糕。你要一些嗎？ wǒ mǎi le yì hé **dàn gāo**. nǐ yào yì xiē ma?
Answer	I'll have one piece, thanks. 我要一塊, 謝謝。 wǒ yào yí kuài, xiè xie

Candy

糖果

táng guǒ

Measure word	顆 kē / 包 bāo
Question	How many candies are in the candy bag? 那包糖裡有幾顆**糖果**？ nà bāo táng lǐ yǒu jǐ kē **táng guǒ**?
Answer	The package says twenty. 包裝說二十顆。 bāo zhuāng shuō èr shí kē

Cheese

乳酪

rǔ luò

Measure word	塊 kuài
Question	Can you get a block of cheese from the store? 你可以從店裡買一塊**乳酪**嗎? nǐ kě yǐ cóng diàn lǐ mǎi yí kuài **rǔ luò** ma?
Answer	What kind of cheese do you want? 你要哪一種**乳酪**? nǐ yào nǎ yì zhǒng **rǔ luò**?

Chocolate

巧克力

qiǎo kè lì

Measure word	塊 kuài / 片 piàn / 條 tiao
Question	Do you want a piece of chocolate? 你要一塊**巧克力**嗎? nǐ yào yí kuài **qiǎo kè lì** ma?
Answer	No, thanks. I don't eat chocolate. 不用,謝謝。我不吃**巧克力**。 bú yòng, xiè xie. wǒ bù chī **qiǎo kè lì**

Coffee

咖啡

kā fēi

Measure word	杯 bēi
Question	Would you like a cup of coffee? 你要一杯咖啡嗎? nǐ yào yì bēi **kā fēi** ma?
Answer	I definitely need a cup of coffee now. 我現在非常需要一杯咖啡。 wǒ xiàn zài fēi cháng xū yào yì bēi **kā fēi**

Cookie

餅乾

bǐng gān

Measure word	包 bāo / 片 piàn
Question	Did you eat the whole bag of cookies? 你把一包餅乾都吃完了? nǐ bǎ yì bāo **bǐng gān** dōu chī wán le?
Answer	There were only three left in the bag! 那包只剩三片而已。 nà bāo zhǐ shèng sān piàn ér yǐ

Egg

蛋

dàn

Measure word	顆 kē / 盒 hé
Question	Do you need a carton of eggs or one egg? 你需要一盒蛋還是一顆蛋？ nǐ xū yào yì hé **dàn** hái shì yì kē **dàn**?
Answer	(I need) just one egg, thanks. 一顆就夠了，謝謝。 yì kē jiù gòu le, xiè xie

Fish

魚

yú

Measure word	條 tiáo
Question	How do you usually cook fish? 你通常如何煮魚？ nǐ tōng cháng rú hé zhǔ **yú**?
Answer	I prefer baking it. 我偏好用烤的。 wǒ piān hào yòng kǎo de

Frozen vegetables

冷凍蔬菜

lěng dòng shū cài

Measure word	包　bāo
Question	What's the benefit of using frozen vegetables? 用**冷凍蔬菜**的好處是什麼？ yòng **lěng dòng shū cài** de hǎo chù shì shén me?
Answer	A bag is cheap, it saves time, and it's healthy. 一包很便宜, 省時間又健康。 yì bāo hěn pián yí, shěng shí jiān yòu jiàn kāng

Ice cream

冰淇淋

bīng qí lín

Measure word	球　qiú / 碗　wǎn
Question	Do you want a scoop of ice cream? 你要一球**冰淇淋**嗎？ nǐ yào yì qiú **bīng qí lín** ma?
Answer	No, I just had a bowl of ice cream. 不用, 我才吃一碗**冰淇淋**。 bú yòng, wǒ cái chī yì wǎn **bīng qí lín**

Juice

果汁

guǒ zhī

Measure word	瓶 píng / 杯 bēi
Question	Would you like a bottle of juice? 你要一瓶**果汁**嗎？ nǐ yào yì píng **guǒ zhī** ma?
Answer	No, I just had a glass of juice at home. 不用，我在家已經喝了一杯**果汁**。 bú yòng, wǒ zài jiā yǐ jīng hē le yì bēi **guǒ zhī**

milk

牛奶

niú nǎi

Measure word	瓶 píng
Question	Do we need to buy a bottle of milk? 我們需要買一瓶**牛奶**嗎？ wǒ men xū yāo mǎi yì píng **niú nǎi** ma?
Answer	No, we still have two bottles at home. 不用，我們還有兩瓶在家。 bú yòng, wǒ men hái yǒu liǎng píng zài jiā

Noodles

miàn

Measure word	包 bāo / 碗 wǎn
Question	Should I buy a bowl of instant noodles or a pack? 我應該買一碗泡**麵**還是一包？ wǒ yīng gāi mǎi yì wǎn pào **miàn** hái shì yì bāo?
Answer	Get both. I like noodles a lot. 兩個都買。我很喜歡**麵**。 liǎng ge dōu mǎi. wǒ hěn xǐ huān **miàn**

Rice

fàn

Measure word	碗 wǎn
Question	Can I have a bowl of rice? 可以給我一碗**飯**嗎？ kě yǐ gěi wǒ yì wǎn **fàn** ma?
Answer	We're out of rice, sorry. 我們沒有**飯**了, 抱歉。 wǒ men méi yǒu **fàn** le, bào qiàn

Salad

沙拉

shā lā

Measure word	碗 wǎn
Question	What's in that bowl of salad? 那碗**沙拉**裡有什麼？ nà wǎn **shā lā** lǐ yǒu shé me?
Answer	I used a lot of organic vegetables. 我用了很多有機蔬菜。 wǒ yòng le hěn duō yǒu jī shū cài

Sandwich

三明治

sān míng zhì

Measure word	個 ge
Question	Can you pack three sandwiches for me? 你能幫我裝三個**三明治**嗎？ nǐ néng bāng wǒ zhuāng sān ge **sān míng zhì** ma?
Answer	Three? Why are you so hungry? 三個?你怎麼這麼餓? sān ge? nǐ zěn me zhè me è?

Soda

qì shuǐ

Measure word	罐 guàn / 瓶 píng
Question	Why do you have a dozen soda? 你為什麼有一打**汽水**？ nǐ wèi shé me yǒu yì dǎ **qì shuǐ**?
Answer	I like to drink a can of soda every day. 我喜歡每天都喝一罐**汽水**。 wǒ xǐ huān měi tiān dōu hè yī guàn **qì shuǐ**

Soup

tāng

Measure word	碗 wǎn
Question	Did you see the bug in your soup? 你看到你那碗**湯**裡有蟲嗎？ nǐ kàn dào nǐ nà wǎn **tāng** lǐ yǒu chóng ma?
Answer	I guess I'll have extra protein. 我想我會有更多蛋白質 wǒ xiǎng wǒ huì yǒu gèng duō dàn bái zhí

Steak

niú pái

Measure word	塊 kuài
Question	How many steaks do we need for tonight? 我們今晚需要幾塊**牛排**？ wǒ men jīn wǎn xū yào jǐ kuài **niú pái**?
Answer	None for me; I'm a vegetarian. 我不用算, 我吃素 wǒ bú yòng suàn, wǒ chī sù

Toast

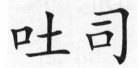

tǔ sī

Measure word	條 tiáo / 片 piàn
Question	How many pieces of toast do you want? 你要幾片**吐司**？ nǐ yào jǐ piàn **tǔ sī**?
Answer	Two pieces is fine, thanks! 兩片就好, 謝謝。 liǎng piàn jiù hǎo, xiè xie

Lesson 9

第九課

dì jiǔ kè

Vegetables

蔬菜

shū cài

Broccoli

綠花椰菜

lǜ huā yé cài

Measure word	顆 kē
Question	Do you like broccoli? 你喜歡**綠花椰菜**嗎？ nǐ xǐ huān **lǜ huā yé cài** ma?
Answer	Yes, broccoli is one of my favorite vegetables. 喜歡,**綠花椰菜**是我最愛的蔬菜之一。 xǐ huān, **lǜ huā yé cài** shì wǒ zuì ài de shū cài zhī yī

Cabbage

高麗菜

gāo lì cài

Measure word	顆 kē
Question	Why is cabbage called "cabbage"? 為什麼**高麗菜**要叫**高麗菜**？ wèi shé me **gāo lì cài** yào jiào **gāo lì cài**?
Answer	I don't know, I'm not a cabbage. 我不知道,我又不是一顆**高麗菜**。 wǒ bù zhī dào, wǒ yòu bú shì yì kē **gāo lì cài**

Carrot

紅蘿蔔

hóng luó bo

Measure word	根 gēn
Question	Did you take my two carrots? 你拿了我的兩根**紅蘿蔔**嗎？ nǐ ná le wǒ de liǎng gēn **hóng luó bo** ma?
Answer	No, I think your rabbit took them. 沒有，我想你的兔子拿走了。 méi yǒu, wǒ xiǎng nǐ de tù zi ná zǒu le

Cauliflower

白花椰菜

bái huā yé cài

Measure word	顆 kē
Question	What dish can you make with cauliflower? 你可以用**白花椰菜**做出什麼料理？ nǐ kě yǐ yòng **bái huā yé cài** zuò chū shén me liào lǐ?
Answer	I can't make anything; I don't know how to cook. 什麼都做不出，我不會煮菜。 shén me dōu zuò bù chū, wǒ bú huì zhǔ cài

Corn

玉米

yù mǐ

Measure word	根 gēn
Question	Don't you think corn looks strange?
	你不覺得**玉米**長的很奇怪嗎？
	nǐ bù jué de **yù mǐ** zhǎng de hěn qí guài ma
Answer	Actually, this cob of corn looks odd.
	說實話, 這根**玉米**看起來怪怪的。
	shuō shí huà, zhè gēn **yù mǐ** kàn qǐ lái guài guài de

Cucumber

小黃瓜

xiǎo huáng guā

Measure word	條 tiáo
Question	Do you put sliced cucumbers on your face?
	你會在臉上放**小黃瓜**切片嗎？
	nǐ huì zài liǎn shàng fàng **xiǎo huáng guā** qiē piàn ma?
Answer	No, I prefer to eat cucumbers.
	不會, 我比較喜歡吃**小黃瓜**。
	bú huì, wǒ bǐ jiào xǐ huān chī **xiǎo huáng guā**

Garlic

大蒜／蒜頭

dà suàn / suàn tóu

Measure word	顆 kē / 瓣 bàn
Question	Why do you smell like garlic? 你為什麼聞起來像**大蒜**？ nǐ wèi shé me wén qǐ lái xiàng **dà suàn**?
Answer	I just ate three cloves of garlic. 我剛剛吃了三瓣**大蒜**。 wǒ gāng gāng chī le sān bàn **dà suàn**

Ginger

jiāng

Measure word	塊 kuài / 片 piàn
Question	How do you use ginger? 你都怎麼使用**薑**？ nǐ dōu zěn me shǐ yòng **jiāng**?
Answer	I always add a piece of ginger in my soup. 我總是在我的湯裡加一片**薑**。 wǒ zǒng shì zài wǒ de tāng lí jiā yī piàn **jiāng**

Lettuce

萵苣

wō jù

Measure word	顆 kē
Question	Do you put lettuce in your burger? 你會放**萵苣**在你的漢堡裡嗎? nǐ huì fàng **wō jù** zài nǐ de hàn bǎo lǐ ma?
Answer	Yes, I put lettuce and sliced tomatoes. 會啊, 我會放**萵苣**和切片番茄。 huì a, wǒ huì fàng **wō jù** hàn qiē piàn fān qié

Mushroom

香菇

xiāng gū

Measure word	朵 duǒ
Question	How many mushrooms do we need? 我們需要幾朵**香菇**? wǒ men xū yào jǐ duǒ **xiāng gū**?
Answer	Maybe five mushrooms. 也許五朵**香菇**。 yě xǔ wǔ duǒ **xiāng gū**

Onion

洋蔥

yáng cōng

Measure word	顆　kē
Question	Do you cry when you cut onions? 你切洋蔥時會哭嗎？ nǐ qiē **yáng cōng** shí huì kū ma?
Answer	No, I wear goggles when cutting onions. 不會, 我切洋蔥會帶護目鏡。 bú huì, wǒ qiē **yáng cōng** huì dài hù mù jìng

Potato

馬鈴薯

mǎ líng shǔ

Measure word	顆　kē / 個　ge
Question	Do you eat a lot of potatoes? 你吃很多馬鈴薯嗎？ nǐ chī hěn duō **mǎ líng shǔ** ma?
Answer	Sometimes I eat two potatoes a day. 有時候我一天吃兩顆馬鈴薯。 yǒu shí hòu wǒ yì tiān chī liǎng kē **mǎ líng shǔ**

Pumpkin

nán guā

Measure word	顆 kē / 個 ge
Question	Why did you buy this pumpkin?
	你為什麼買這顆**南瓜**？
	nǐ wèi shé me mǎi zhè kē **nán guā**?
Answer	I want to make a pumpkin pie.
	我要做一個**南瓜**派。
	wǒ yào zuò yí ge **nán guā** pài

Spring onion

cōng

Measure word	把 bǎ / 根 gēn
Question	Why did you get this bunch of spring onions?
	你為什麼拿這麼大把**蔥**？
	nǐ wèi shé me ná zhè me dà bǎ **cōng**
Answer	I need two spring onions to make lunch.
	我需要兩根**蔥**來做午餐。
	wǒ xū yào liǎng gēn **cōng** lái zuò wǔ cān

Lesson 10
第十課
dì shí kè

Zoo Animals
動物園動物
dòng wù yuán dòng wù

Bear

熊

xióng

Measure word	隻 zhī
Question	Do you know why polar bears are endangered? 你知道為什麼北極**熊**快絕種嗎？ nǐ zhī dào běi jí **xióng** kuài jué zhǒng ma?
Answer	It might be that they drink too much cola. 可能是他們喝太多可樂。 kě néng shì tā men hē tài duō kě lè

Camel

駱駝

luò tuó

Measure word	隻 zhī
Question	Why does your camel keep drooling? 你那隻**駱駝**為什麼一直流口水？ nǐ nà zhī **luò tuó** wèi shé me yì zhí liú kǒu shuǐ?
Answer	I'm not sure, maybe that's its hobby. 不確定,也許那是牠的嗜好。 bú què dìng, yě xǔ nà shì tā de shì hào

Elephant

dà xiàng

Measure word	隻 zhī / 頭 tóu
Question	Do you know how big an elephant can grow?
	你知道一隻**大象**能長多大嗎？
	nǐ zhī dào yì zhī **dà xiàng** néng zhǎng duō dà ma?
Answer	No, but that one over there is pretty big.
	不知道, 但那邊那隻蠻大的。
	bù zhī dào, dàn nà biān nà zhī mán dà de

Giraffe

長頸鹿

cháng jǐng lù

Measure word	隻 zhī
Question	Can you run faster than a giraffe?
	你能跑得比**長頸鹿**快嗎？
	nǐ néng pǎo dé bǐ **cháng jǐng lù** kuài ma?
Answer	No way I can outrun a giraffe.
	我是不可能跑得過**長頸鹿**的。
	wǒ shì bù kě néng pǎo de guò **cháng jǐng lù** de

Hippo

河馬

hé mǎ

Measure word	隻 zhī / 頭 tóu
Question	What are those two hippos doing? 那兩隻**河馬**在做什麼？ nà liǎng zhī **hé mǎ** zài zuò shén me
Answer	One is swimming, the other is eating. 一隻在游泳，一隻在吃東西。 yì zhī zài yóu yǒng, yì zhī zài chī dōng xī

Horse

馬

mǎ

Measure word	匹 pī
Question	Have you ridden a horse before? 你有騎過**馬**嗎？ nǐ yǒu qí guò **mǎ** ma?
Answer	No, but I've fed a herd of horses. 沒有，但我有餵過一群**馬**。 méi yǒu, dàn wǒ yǒu wèi guò yì qún **mǎ**

Kangaroo

袋鼠

dài shǔ

Measure word	隻 zhī
Question	Why was that kangaroo so angry? 那隻**袋鼠**為什麼這麼生氣？ nà zhī **dài shǔ** wèi shé me zhè me shēng qì?
Answer	Someone got too close to its baby. 有人太接近它的寶寶。 yǒu rén tài jiē jìn tā de bǎo bao

Koala

無尾熊

wú wěi xióng

Measure word	隻 zhī
Question	Have you held a koala? 你抱過**無尾熊**嗎？ nǐ bào guò **wú wěi xióng** ma?
Answer	Yes, a koala is actually very heavy. 有，**無尾熊**其實很重。 yǒu, **wú wěi xióng** qí shí hěn zhòng

Lion

獅子

shī zi

Measure word	隻 zhī
Question	How loud can a lion roar? 獅子能吼多大聲？ **shī zi** néng hǒu duō dà shēng?
Answer	Lions roar louder than any other big cats. 獅子吼的比任何其他大貓大聲。 **shī zi** hǒu de bǐ rèn hé qí tā dà māo dà shēng

Monkey

猴子

hóu zi

Measure word	隻 zhī
Question	What does a monkey like to eat? 猴子喜歡吃什麼？ **hóu zi** xǐ huān chī shén me?
Answer	Monkeys actually like to eat insects. 猴子其實喜歡吃昆蟲。 **hóu zi** qí shí xǐ huān chī kūn chóng

Panda

貓熊

māo xióng

Measure word	隻 zhī
Question	How many pandas are at this zoo? 這個動物園裡有幾隻**貓熊**? zhè ge dòng wù yuán lǐ yǒu jǐ zhī **māo xióng**?
Answer	Last time I came there were two pandas. 上次我來時有兩隻**貓熊**。 shàng cì wǒ lái shí yǒu liǎng zhī **māo xióng**

Rhino

犀牛

xī niú

Measure word	隻 zhī / 頭 tóu
Question	Do rhinos sleep standing up? **犀牛**站著睡覺嗎? **xī niú** zhàn zhe shuì jiào ma?
Answer	I have no idea; I don't know much about rhinos. 不知道,我不太了解**犀牛**。 bù zhī dào, wǒ bú tài liǎo jiě **xīn iú**

Snake

蛇

shé

Measure word	條 tiáo
Question	Which kind of snake is the most dangerous? 哪一種**蛇**最危險？ nǎ yì zhǒng **shé** zuì wéi xiǎn?
Answer	I'm not sure, but I'm afraid of all snakes. 不確定,但我什麼**蛇**都怕。 bú què dìng, dàn wǒ shén me **shé** dōu pà

Tiger

老虎

lǎo hǔ

Measure word	隻 zhī
Question	How high can a tiger jump? **老虎**能跳多高？ **lǎo hǔ** néng tiào duō gāo?
Answer	I'm sure tigers jump much higher than you can. 我確定**老虎**能跳的比你高。 wǒ què dìng **lǎo hǔ** néng tiào de bǐ nǐ gāo.

Zebra

斑馬

bān mǎ

Measure word	匹 pī
Question	Why do zebras have stripes?
	為什麼**斑馬**有條紋？
	wèi shé me **bān mǎ** yǒu tiáo wén?
Answer	Hmm...because they understand fashion?
	嗯. . .因為他們懂流行？
	en... yīn wèi tā men dǒng liú xíng?

Noun Reference List

-------------------------- A --------------------------

Airplane	飛機	fēi jī		Apartment	公寓	gōng yù
Apple	蘋果	píng guǒ				

-------------------------- B --------------------------

Banana	香蕉	xiāng jiāo		Bathtub	浴缸	yù gāng
Bear	熊	xióng		Bicycle	腳踏車	jiǎo tà chē
Blanket	毛毯	máo tǎn		Blender	果汁機	guǒ zhī jī
Boarding pass	登機證	dēng jī zhèng		Bottle opener	開瓶器	kāi píng qì
Bottled water	瓶裝水	píng zhuāng shuǐ		Bowl	碗	wǎn
Broccoli	綠花椰菜	lǜ huā yé cài		Burger	漢堡	hàn bǎo
Bus stop	公車站牌	gōng chē zhàn				

-------------------------- C --------------------------

Cabbage	高麗菜	gāo lì cài		Cake	蛋糕	dàn gāo
Calculator	計算機	jì suàn jī		Camel	駱駝	luò tuó
Candy	糖果	táng guǒ		Car	汽車	qì chē
Carrot	紅蘿蔔	hóng luó bo		Carry-on Luggage	隨身行李	suí shēn xíng lǐ
Cauliflower	白花椰菜	bái huā yé cài		Chair	椅子	yǐ zi
Cheese	乳酪	rǔ luò		Cherry	櫻桃	yīng táo
Chicken	雞	jī		Chocolate	巧克力	qiǎo kè lì
Chopsticks	筷子	kuài zi		Coconut	椰子	yé zi
Coffee	咖啡	kā fēi		Coffee maker	咖啡機	kā fēi jī
Computer	電腦	diàn nǎo		Conditioner	潤髮乳	rùn fǎ rǔ
Cookie	餅乾	bǐng gān		Copy machine	影印機	yǐng yìn jī
Corn	玉米	yù mǐ		Correction fluid	修正液	xiū zhèng yì
Cotton swab	棉花棒	mián huā bàng		Counter	櫃檯	guì tái
Cow	乳牛	rǔ niú		Cucumber	小黃瓜	xiǎo huáng guā
Cup	杯子	bēi zi				

-------------------------- D --------------------------

Dog	狗	gǒu		Donkey	驢子	lǘ zi
Duck	鴨子	yā zi				

-------------------------------- E --------------------------------

Egg	蛋	dàn		Electric razor	電動刮鬍刀	diàn dòng guā hú dāo
Elephant	大象	dà xiàng		Extension cord	延長線	yán cháng xiàn

-------------------------------- F --------------------------------

Faucet	水龍頭	shuǐ lóng tóu		Fish	魚	yú
Flight attendant	空服員	kōng fú yuán		Folder	資料夾	zī liào jiá
Fork	叉子	chā zi		Frozen vegetables	冷凍蔬菜	lěng dòng shū cài

-------------------------------- G --------------------------------

Garlic	大蒜/蒜頭	dà suàn / suàn tóu		Gate	登機門	dēng jī mén
Ginger	薑	jiāng		Giraffe	長頸鹿	cháng jǐng lù
Glass	玻璃杯	bō lí bēi		Glue	膠水	jiāo shuǐ
Goat	山羊	shān yáng		Grapefruit	葡萄柚	pú táo yòu
Grapes	葡萄	pú táo				

-------------------------------- H --------------------------------

Hairdryer	吹風機	chuī fēng jī		Highlighter	螢光筆	yíng guāng bǐ
Hippo	河馬	hé mǎ		Horse	馬	mǎ

-------------------------------- I --------------------------------

Ice cream	冰淇淋	bīng qí lín	

-------------------------------- K --------------------------------

Kangaroo	袋鼠	dài shǔ		Keyboard	鍵盤	jiàn pán
Knife	刀子	dāo zi		Koala	無尾熊	wú wěi xióng

-------------------------------- L --------------------------------

Lemon	檸檬	níng méng		Letter	信	xìn
Lettuce	萵苣	wō jù		Lid	蓋子	gài zi
Light / lamp	燈	dēng		Lion	獅子	shī zi
Luggage	行李	xíng lǐ				

-------------------------------- M --------------------------------

Marker	馬克筆	mǎ kè bǐ		Milk	牛奶	niú nǎi
Mirror	鏡子	jìng zi		Monkey	猴子	hóu zi

Motorcycle	機車	jī chē		Mushroom	香菇	xiāng gū

-------------------------- **N** --------------------------

Napkin	餐巾紙	cān jīn zhǐ		Noodles	麵	miàn
Notebook	筆記本	bǐ jì běn				

-------------------------- **O** --------------------------

Onion	洋蔥	yáng cōng		Orange	柳橙	liǔ chéng
Oven	烤箱	kǎo xiāng				

-------------------------- **P** --------------------------

Panda	貓熊	māo xióng		Paper	紙	zhǐ
Paper clip	迴紋針	huí wén zhēn		Parking lot	停車場	tíng chē chǎng
Passport	護照	hù zhào		Peach	水蜜桃	shuǐ mì táo
Pear	梨子	lí zi		Pen	筆	bǐ
Perfume	香水	xiāng shuǐ		Phone	電話	diàn huà
Pig	豬	zhū		Pineapple	鳳梨	fèng lí
Plate	盤子	pán zi		Post-it	便利貼	biàn lì tiē
Pot	鍋子	guō zi		Potato	馬鈴薯	mǎ líng shǔ
Pumpkin	南瓜	nán guā				

-------------------------- **R** --------------------------

Rabbit	兔子	tù zi		Rat	老鼠	lǎo shǔ
Razor	刮鬍刀	guā hú dāo		Rhino	犀牛	xī niú
Rice	飯	fàn		Road	路	lù
Rubber band	橡皮筋	xiàng pí jīn				

-------------------------- **S** --------------------------

Salad	沙拉	shā lā		Sandwich	三明治	sān míng zhì
Seat	座位	zuò wèi		Seat belt	安全帶	ān quán dài
Shampoo	洗髮精	xǐ fǎ jīng		Sheep	綿羊	mián yang
Shower head	蓮蓬頭	lián peng tóu		Shuttle bus	接駁巴士	jiē bó bā shì
Skillet	煎鍋	jiān guō		Skyscraper	摩天大樓	mó tiān dà lóu
Snake	蛇	shé		Soap	肥皂	féi zào
Soda	汽水	qì shuǐ		Soup	湯	tang
Sponge	海綿	hǎi mián		Spoon	湯匙	tāng chí
Spring onion	蔥	cōng		Stamp / seal	印章	yìn zhāng
Stapler	釘書機	dìng shū jī		Steak	牛排	niú pái

Store	商店	shāng diàn		Strawberry	草莓	cǎo méi
Street	街	jiē				

-------------------------- **T** --------------------------

Table	桌子	zhuō zi		Tangerine	橘子	jú zi
Tape	膠帶	jiāo dài		Taxi	計程車	jì chéng chē
Terminal	航廈	háng shà		Ticket	票	piào
Tiger	老虎	lǎo hǔ		Tile	磁磚	cí zhuān
Tissue	衛生紙	wèi shēng zhǐ		Toast	吐司	tǔ sī
Toaster	烤麵包機	kǎo miàn bāo jī		Tooth brush	牙刷	yá shuā
Toothpaste	牙膏	yá gāo		Towel	毛巾	máo jīn
Traffic light	紅綠燈	hóng lǜ dēng		Turkey	火雞	huǒ jī

-------------------------- **V** --------------------------

Visa	簽證	qiān zhèng	

-------------------------- **W** --------------------------

Watermelon	西瓜	xī guā	

-------------------------- **Z** --------------------------

Zebra	斑馬	bān mǎ	

Made in United States
North Haven, CT
27 December 2023

46677990R00068